I AM BRILLIANT

Laura Clemons
Gavin Moore
Micah Moore

I AM BRILLIANT

Printed in the United States of America

ISBN: 978-0-578-35542-9

DEDICATION

In Loving Memory Of My Parents- Willie and Velma Clemons

David Laren Johnson
Loved Always

Psalms 46

God is my refuge and my strength, my help for all troubles.

Psalms 119 verse 133

Order my steps in thy word: and let not any iniquity have control over me.

Philippians 4

Let all men see that you are good gentle and kind. Don't worry, pray and Ask God for what you need.

Table of Contents

CHAPTER 1

I AM BRILLIANT - The Lawyer / Juvenile Court Referee

B - Black and Brave

R - Resilient, Respectful

I - Incredible, Intelligent

L - Loving Leader

L - Lady, Laughter

I - Industrious

A - Abundance of joy

N - Nice, Noble

T - Truthful, Thankful

I AM BRILLIANT- BLACK AND BRAVE

I am a brilliant black woman who is an attorney.

I became a brilliant attorney because there are few African American women attorneys.

I am brilliant in that I became an attorney after my first career as a social worker and grief counselor.

I use my brave skills to help children remain protected in their homes or the care of others. I opened The Clemons Law Firm, LLC in 2009 - September 30, 2021.

October 1, 2021, I became the Juvenile Court Referee in Montgomery, Alabama. I am glad that God is ordering my steps.

"Order my steps in thy word; and let not any iniquity have dominion over me." Psalms 119:133.

"The steps of a good man are ordered by the Lord and he delighteth in His way." Psalms 37:23.

I AM BRILLIANT – RESILIENT, RESPECTFUL

Becoming an attorney and opening my law firm required respect for myself, others, and the judicial system. I respect the persons I represent and fight for their rights.

I am resilient. I became an attorney while working to send my children to college. I worked part-time, attended law school, and studied at night.

My son died right before my graduation. Yet, I did not give up. I asked God to help me stay on the path He has for me. God gave me strength and made me resilient.

I passed the bar exam and entered the real world of helping others with legal matters. It was hard financing my firm at first. I started in my home office, and God blessed me with clients.

I AM BRILLIANT- INCREDIBLE, INTELLIGENT

Being incredibly brilliant and intelligent is truly a gift from God. God has given me traits and skills that I do not take for granted throughout my educational career. I never settled for "I can't." My God, parents, and some teachers encouraged me to accomplish greatness.

I always prayed, studied hard, and excelled academically.

As a young black girl, I attended integrated schools in the late 60s-70s. Facing racism, discrimination, and hateful treatment made me incredibly strong and determined to succeed. One of my high school teachers told me I should not attend the University of Alabama but should attend a school with "my kind." Look at what God has done!

I graduated from Tuscaloosa Jr. High and Tuscaloosa High on the honor roll and became a member of the National Honor Society. God allowed me to graduate with honors and cum laude from the University of Alabama with a BSW and MSW.

Then God allowed me to graduate from the Birmingham School of Law and open my law firm. The Clemons Law Firm, LLC. Now God has allowed me to become a full-time juvenile court referee. I am following the steps that God has for me.

I cannot be afraid and run like Jonah, and I cannot be angry like Naomi. I have tasted and seen that the Lord is good. He is my strength and refuge. He has plans to prosper and not harm me. I am a chosen child of the King.

I AM A BRILLIANT LOVING LEADER

Growing up, my parents taught me to love God and others. My dad told me to treat others the way I want to be treated. My mom told me to always pray and experience my role as a loving and kind leader.

My dad worked at a sawmill and sold wood and coal to the neighbors. My mother was a homemaker and ran a home daycare. I remember that our house was a gathering place. We were poor and always had enough to feed guests and visitors. My mother taught me to love our caucasian neighbors who lived on one side of the street and we on the other side. We spoke and waved but never played together.

I remember shopping with my mom and entering through the store's back door to purchase shoes. My mom looked sad when I asked why we were entering the back door. She just said, "One day, you will understand, and one day you will be the owner of a business." My mom spoke my business into existence. I saw how my mom took the lead to make sure we were dressed nicely and worked hard in school. She taught us that failure is not an option.

My dad was also a great leader. He could not read, and I asked why. He said he had to work and quit school to help his parents work.

Later, my dad and I enrolled in adult night school. He went to school, and I was allowed to sit in class with him. I helped my dad learn to read and write and add and subtract. When he graduated, I was so proud of him. He was determined to learn, and I was determined to help him. I was so proud of my dad at his graduation. My mom made me a new dress, and I walked with him to get his diploma. We were walking and crying together. My mom and sibling smiled, and then we went for ice cream afterward. That was the day I said I would never stop learning.

Lessons My Parents taught me:

1. Work hard and always pray.
2. Never give up.
3. Show God how you love Him by doing the right thing all the time. If you lie, go back and tell the truth.
4. Forgive yourself.
5. Be kind even if others are not kind to you.
6. Dress up and always put on your lipstick.
7. Read your Bible every day.

I AM BRILLIANT- LADY, LAUGHTER

I am a brilliant lady with laughter. Laughter makes the world a better place. I bring fun and laughter to my work. "Then our mouth was filled with laughter, and our tongue with shouts of joy; then it was said among the nations, the Lord has done remarkable things for them." Psalms 126:2

We were always laughing at my house. The funniest thing that I remember laughing about was trying to smoke. I played with the neighbor's son, and he tried to teach me to smoke. I did not know how to blow the smoke out, and it went down my throat. I choked and felt sick to my stomach. I ran home to tell my mother, then decided not to. I would have gotten a spanking. So, I drank a gallon of water to get the smoke out of me. I thought that the smoke would damage my throat and lungs. So later, I laughed about it and never touched another cigarette. My parents never knew, and I did not smoke again. I don't think I played with the young man again, either.

Today I enjoy playing and laughing with my two wonderful grandsons, Gavin and Micah.

I AM BRILLIANT- INDUSTRIOUS

God wants me to work hard and help others. I love the scripture that says,

"The thoughts of the industrious always bring forth abundance; but every sluggard is always in want." Proverbs 21:5. I am a brilliant and industrious woman.

While growing up, my first job was babysitting and helping one of my teachers with her housework. One summer, I made enough money to help buy our school supplies and Christmas presents. I was elated to have my money.

At sixteen, my sister and I bought our first car. My dad signed for us, and we made monthly payments. My sister could not drive, so I became her "Driving Ms. Dorothy." Gas was twenty-five cents a gallon, and I thought that was a lot.

I worked throughout high school, college, graduate school and law school. I enjoy helping others and sharing the funds God gives me with others.

I AM BRILLIANT- ABUNDANCE OF JOY

I have an abundance of joy. "For in a severe test of affliction, their abundance of joy and their extreme poverty have overflowed in a wealth of generosity on their part." 2 Corinthians 8:2.

I have learned to have abundant joy as a brilliant person living for God.

I AM BRILLIANT- NICE, NOBLE

I am a brilliant, nice, and noble person. No matter how others treat me, I will remain kind and nice. I pray for the persons who were not kind to me and ask God to forgive them and me for our sins. Forgiveness of myself and others leads me to become spiritually nice and noble. "Be kind to one another, tenderhearted, forgiving one another, as God in Christ forgave you."

"Therefore, as God's chosen people, holy and dearly loved, clothe yourselves with compassion, kindness, humility, gentleness and patience." Colossians 3-12.

I AM BRILLIANT- TRUTHFUL, THANKFUL

As a brilliant, kind, beautiful black woman, I am truthful and thankful.

"Teach me your way, O Lord, that I may walk in your truth; unite my heart to fear your name."

"Do not be anxious about anything, but in everything by prayer and supplications with thanksgiving let your supplication with thanksgiving let your requests be made known to God." Philippians 4:6.

I am thankful to God the Father, God the Son and God the Holy Spirit for my life of service to God and others. I am truly blessed, brilliant and thankful to have written my first book.

I pray that my book and short stories of my life will encourage other brown skin children to dream big, trust God and never give up. Allow God to order your steps to be brilliant and blessed.

CHAPTER 2

I AM BRILLIANT - The Basketball Player

B - Bright, Brave, Beloved,

R - Respectful, Reliable, Responsible, Righteous

I - Intelligent, Ideal, Incredible, Imaginative, Independent, Impressive

L - Leader, Loving

L - Learner, Loyal

I - Inspired

A - Ambitious, Accepting, Amazing, Amusing, Appreciative, Astonishing

N - Nice, Neat, Noble

T - Talented, Thankful

I AM BRILLIANT

I am a bright basketball player.

I am a brave basketball player.

I am a beloved basketball player.

I am a brilliant basketball player.

I AM BRILLIANT

I am a respectful basketball player.

I am a reliable basketball player.

I am a responsible basketball player.

I am a righteous basketball player.

I AM A BRILLIANT

I am an intelligent basketball player.

I am an ideal basketball player.

I am an incredible basketball player.

I am an imaginative basketball player.

I am an independent basketball player.

I am an impressive basketball player.

I AM BRILLIANT

I am a leader because I lead by example. I am also a great leader because I show my team good sportsmanship. I am a loving basketball player and a loving person. I am a lovable basketball player because I care about my coaches, teammates and family.

I AM BRILLIANT

I will learn different moves with people who want to play basketball in training.

I am loyal because I believe in my team every game.

I am an important basketball player.

I believe in accepting challenges that may seem impossible.

I am inspired by some magical skills NBA players use.

I AM BRILLIANT

I am an ambitious basketball player.

I am an accepting basketball player.

I am an amazing basketball player.

I am an amusing basketball player.

I am an appreciative basketball player.

I am an astonishing basketball player.

I AM BRILLIANT

I am a nice basketball player.

I am a neat basketball player.

I am a noble basketball player.

I AM BRILLIANT

I am a talented basketball player because I have a lot of talent.

I am a thankful basketball player because God has given me great skills, and I will use them wisely.

CHAPTER 3

I AM BRILLIANT - The Doctor

B - Brave, Beloved

R - Responsible, Reliable

I - Intelligent, Impressive, Independent

L - Learner, Leader

L - Loving, Loyal

I - Incredible, Innovative

A - Ambitious, Amazing, Awesome, Appreciative

N - Nice

T - Talented, Thankful

I AM BRILLIANT

I am going to become a brilliant doctor. I am brave now and will start studying to be the best-beloved doctor. I am a brilliant doctor.

I AM BRILLIANT

I am going to become a responsible and reliable doctor.

My patients can rely on me to give them the best care available.

I am a brilliant doctor.

I AM BRILLIANT

I will become an intelligent doctor. I will say, "I am an impressive, intelligent and independent doctor."

I am a brilliant doctor.

I AM BRILLIANT

I will learn to become a doctor at a major medical school.

I will be a brilliant leader as a doctor. I will discover new medical cures.

I am a brilliant doctor.

I AM BRILLIANT

I will become a brilliant doctor. "I am a loving doctor. I help my patients get well."

I am loyal to my patients, and their well-being is most important.

I am a brilliant doctor.

I am an incredible doctor.

I believe in hard work to become an innovative doctor.

I am a brilliant doctor.

I AM BRILLIANT

I am an ambitious, amazing and awesome doctor.

I appreciate my granny, brother, mother and father for supporting me in becoming a doctor.

I am a brilliant doctor.

I AM BRILLIANT

I am a nice doctor. I listen to my patients. I care.

I am a brilliant doctor.

I AM BRILLIANT

I am a talented doctor. I am thankful because God has blessed me with great skills. I will use them wisely.

I am a brilliant doctor.

Describe How Brilliant You Are!!!

I Am Brilliant.

B____

R____

I____

L____

L____

I____

A____

N____

T____

MEET THE AUTHORS

www.ingramcontent.com/pod-product-compliance
Lightning Source LLC
LaVergne TN
LVHW070205110826
845147LV00002B/510

* 9 7 8 0 5 7 8 3 5 5 4 2 9 *